Learn WordPress
Second Edition

Inderjeet Singh

CONTENTS

Title Page	
WORDPRESS	1
WORDPRESS INSTALLATION	2
WORDPRESS MENUS	5
WORDPRESS HOOKS	19
MAKE A WORDPRESS PLUGIN	26
IMPORTANT FUNCTIONS	31
IMPORTANT FILES	40
CREATE CUSTOM TEMPLATE AND MENU	48
MAKING CUSTOM CODED WEBSITE MENU DYNAMIC	60
API INTEGRATIONS	65
Thank You	91

WORDPRESS

WordPress is a CMS (Content management system). We can make websites in WordPress. It allow us to use readymade themes, plugins and to work on them only using menus rather than working on coding. Sometimes we also need to do some coding in WordPress to solve some issues or to add some special functionality. We will learn both in this book - menus as well as coding part in WordPress.

HISTORY OF WORDPRESS

WordPress was born out of a desire for an elegant, well-architectured personal publishing system built on PHP and MySQL and licensed under the GPL. It is the official successor of b2/cafelog. WordPress is modern software, but its roots and development go back to 2001. It is a mature and stable product.

WORDPRESS INSTALLATION

1) WordPress' latest version can be downloaded at https://wordpress.org/download/ .

2) Downloaded zip file needs a server. It could be either a live paid web server such as hostripplies.com, bluehost.com, etc. or a free localhost web server such as XAMPP. XAMPP can be downloaded at https://filehippo.com/download_xampp/ .

[You can install WordPress on your computer, on your bought hosting server or free online servers are also available with limited facilities to host your website.]

3) Once our web server is ready, we can unzip (or extract) the downloaded WordPress file in it.

a) On live server, WordPress zip file need to be extracted for usage. WordPress unzipped files can be placed inside Cpanel > File Manager > public_html folder. Live server should be pointing to a bought domain name or URL, such as https://ziscom.in. If you do not have a domain name, it can be bought from https://namecheap.com, etc. and link to your hosting by setting nameservers. You should also create a database on your hosting and note the database name, username and password and find the wp-config.php file in 'public_html' folder and enter these details in appropriate places in code. WordPress files extracted inside public_html folder can be run in web browser by entering the set domain name (or website URL). When you run your domain name (website name) first time in browser, it will ask you enter website title, your email, WordPress website's new password, etc. And it will install the WordPress on live server.

b) In case of local server, XAMPP can be started from file at C:\xampp\xampp-control. WordPress downloaded zipped file can be unzipped using Winrar software [You can get it free here: https://ziscom.in/free-softwares/]. Unzipped WordPress folder need to be placed inside 'htdocs' folder which can be found in XAMPP folder installation at path C:\xampp\htdocs. Name of folder which contains extracted WordPress becomes the local domain name. e.g. our unzipped WordPress files are placed inside folder named mysite, so, in web browser like chrome, etc. enter localhost/mysite to see output. We need to set up database as well. For setting database enter localhost/phpmyadmin in your browser. [Remember to save all the created username, database name, password, etc. details safely for later use.] and put them in wp-config.php file as required in code. Once it is done, WordPress can be installed locally at path localhost/mysite. It will ask you to provide website tile, email, WordPress website password, etc. Once setup completes, you can run the website locally and edit it.

Here I am also adding a separate step of how to create a database:

a) If on live server, database can be created in Cpanel > Databases > MySQL Database Wizard. First enter database name, then username and password. Password should be mixture of letters, Capital letter, numbers and alphanumeric with atleast 5 characters long. Once you created database, note these details. These details asked when we click on browser domain name as exlained above or we need to put them in wp-config.php file inside WordPress extracted folder.

b) In case of local server activate XAMPP. Go to web browser and type localhost/phpmyadmin. It opens database list infront of you. You can create a database. By default localhost database username is 'root' and password is empty ". You database is made, you can put database name, database username and database password inside localhost/Wordpress installation or in wp-config.php file insize C:\xampp\htdocs\wordpress\wp-config.php file.

[All this is a very simple process. Once you install it once or twice yourself, you do not need to look at the installation process again and you can do it yourself easily. If you need any help, you can contact me at ziscom18@gmail.com, I am available to hire, for an advice at a minimal price of few dollars.]

WORDPRESS MENUS

Once you have completed installing WordPress on live server or localhost as mentioned in earlier chapter. Login to your WordPress and now WordPress is all about menus. Whole of the website can be made using WordPress menus without touching the code. To login to your WordPress once you have set it up successfully you need to enter this url in web browser, www.domainname.com/ wp-admin. In case of localhost you enter localhost/domain- name.com/wp-admin. After it enter your WordPress login details in it. It will open a window like this:

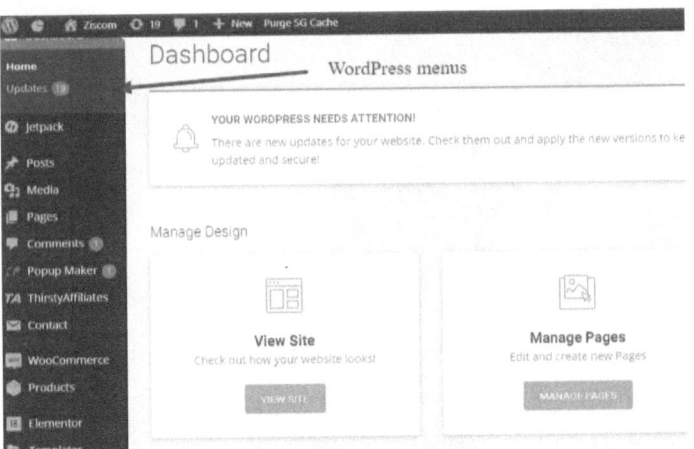

Once you reach this page it means you are ready to start making website in WordPress now. Before actually starting to make a Website, let us study what are WordPress menus. You can see in the left of page there is black stripe and it contains various WordPress menus. Let us study them one by one.

1) Dashboard: - It is the first page which opens after login. It contains some important menus, notifications, useful links according to WordPress.

2) Posts: - A post is a website page which contains date, author, etc. details within it whoever write it. Anyone visiting your website can write comments below your post. All the posts made one by one can be fetched in chronological order in a di9erent web page or a 'blog' page. We can assign di9erent categories or tags to posts and show particular category of posts at one place and other category of posts under some other topic. When we move mouse icon on 'Posts' menu it show us four sub- options, 'All Posts', 'Add New', 'Categories' and 'Tags'.

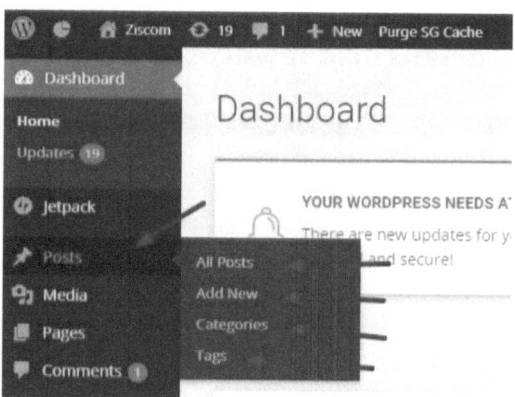

a) All Posts: - When we click on it, it shows list of all the made posts so far. When we move mouse on any post, it shows sub-menu linked to it as shown in image:

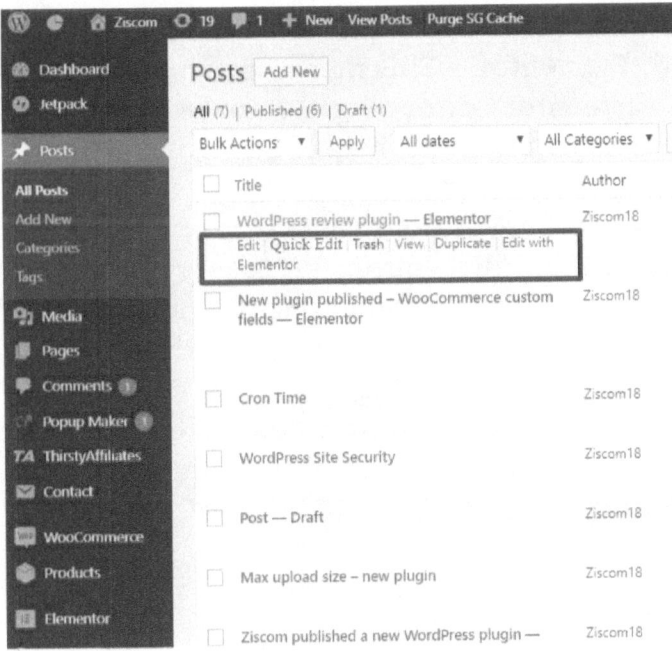

Image above shows 'All Posts' and it is showing sub-menu in blue rectangle when we move mouse pointer on a post name. It has multiple submenus,

i) Edit: - To edit post.

ii) Quick Edit: - It opens another sub-sub menu where we can change title of post, slug of post, category of post, apply tags to post, add password to post, etc. without actually opening post through edit.

iii) Trash: - It is used to delete the post.

iv) View: - It is used to view the published page made so far.

v) Duplicate: - This option has been added here using 'Duplicate WordPress elements' plugin, it can be used to create a duplicate post for new post with similar design as current one or for testing purpose.

vi) Edit with Elementor: - This menu option is showing because of installed 'Elementor' editor plugin. It make it easy for us to edit page design if we edit with the help of Elementor.

[There are many other editors available. Most important of them are 'gutenburg editor', 'divi editor', 'WPBakery', etc. We can install them through plugin, some come free in WordPress themes. We will study about plugins and themes later in the book.]

b) Add New: - It allow us to make a new post. When we click on this menu option, it opens a page in front of us where we can enter our page title, text, etc.

Here you can see post page. It has multiple sub-menus inside it.

i) Edit Post: - You can enter title of post here.

ii) Permalink: - You can make your post's permalink here. Permalink refers to the web url. For example, if you enter here 'new', your this post can be seen after publishing at web url path: https://www.yourdomain/new

iii) Editor: - You can enter post text in area below it. It is showing option to edit with Elimentor or WordPress Editor.

iv) Screen Options: - On top-right corner there is menu, where you can select various menus which you want to use and will be displayed in this page. It can be used to show list of post published previously, so that if current version of post has some error, we can set to previous version of post.

v) Publish: - There is a 'Publish' button in blue color on right side of image. Once your post is ready, you can publish it by clicking this button to make it visible live with latest changes.

vi) Categories: - You can select categories for post as shown arrow in bottom right corner of post.

[Image shown above have many other menus, we are pointing out most important ones. We can select menu options to make our post like that. They are self explanatery and easy to understand mostly when we visit this page or are rarely used so we can ignore them for now and when need, we can search online at https://google.com for them to get more details about them. These post menus keep changing in di9erent versions of WordPress. To see it exactly as shown here install plugin 'Classic editor'. We will study about how to install plugin later. For now you can study the whatever latest post version shows up. It should have these important menus linked as explained above.]

c) Categories: - It allows you to make di9erent categories which you can assign to your posts. Image above shows,

i) Name: - Top left text field to enter new category name.

ii) Slug: - Slug is the part of web url path. For example, if we enter slug here, 'work'. And we assign some posts this category with slug 'work'. We can see all those posts with category 'new' at url https://www.yourdomain/category/work/

iii) Parent category: - If we made a category already and we want to assign current category as sub-category, we can select name of parent category here.

iv) Description: - We can write our category description here, or we can also leave it empty.

v) Add new category: - This button is used to create the category based on above details entered.

vi) Category list: - On right side, we see list of categories already made.

Once you make a category here, you can assign it to a post. We can assign category to a post from inside the post edit page, as shown in image below:

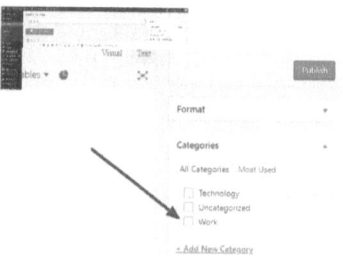

It can be assigned from 'Quick Edit' menu as well as explained before.

d) Tags: - Tags are similar to categories. We make them same way and assign them to posts by writing name of made tag. They are rarely used. They can be used, if we want to assign some posts to a particular category however also want to enlist it another list so we can make and assign tag to that post.

3. Media: - It keeps all the images, songs, videos, zip files, etc. we will be using in our Website. First we upload our image file to WordPress Media, then use it in website posts, pages, etc. created in WordPress.

[Sometimes we want to upload bigger size files in Media and they fail to upload because of the default limit set on upload size. We can increase upload size for bigger files using plugin 'Max upload size']

4) Pages: - It is the website pages we make here. Similar to Posts, Pages also have a 'Quick Edit' menu with similar options however we can not set category or tags for a page. When we click on 'Add New' button in 'Pages' menu it shows a window similar to 'Post' Edit menu studied above. Let us study about 'Page Editor', as it is important part of a page.

a) Page Editor: - Here is the image:

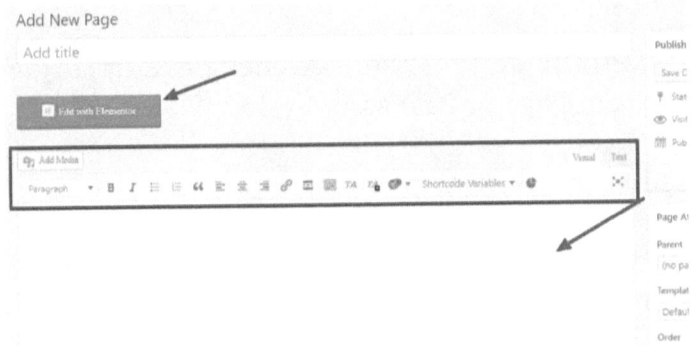

Here we are showing example of 'Classic Editor' which can be downloaded through 'Plugin menu'. There a lot of editors available as discussed before. Image above shows, we can choose 'Elementor' as editor to edit. Which contains a lot of other easy to understand menus to quickly design page. In blue rectangle is the various options to edit the text. It includes putting a media file in text area shown. Making text bold, underline, italic, change font, color, size of text, etc. In right side of rectable shown there is option two tabs 'Visual' and 'Text'. In 'Text' we can write our HTML and CSS and when we click on 'Visual' tab, it shows us output.

b) Publish menu: - Now, let us study 'Publish' menu in detail as it is also a useful menu.

Publish menu has multiple options, let us study them one by one.

i) Save Draft: - When we add something to the Page or Post, we can save it in the form of draft so that we can continue work on it next time we come to edit it.

ii) Preview: - It is used to preview the page how it will look like on live website after publishing it. However we do not publish it yet and preview output by click 'Preview' button.

iii) Status: Draft Edit: - When we click on 'Edit', it give us option to select 'Draft' or 'Pending Review'.

iv) Visibility: Public Edit: - When we click on 'Edit', it give us option to set current Page or Post as

'Public' - visible to all after publish,

'Password Protected' - Need to enter a password to view published page or

'Private' - Page is visible only to administrator after login to WordPress.

v) Publish Immediately Edit: - When we click on 'Edit' it allow us to publish the page at a particular date, hours and minutes. We can create the Page or Post and set it to publish automatically at a later date and time.

vi) Publish: - Blue 'Publish' button allow us to publish the page immediately and whatever changes we make on page becomes live on website immediately.

c) Page Attributes: - Another important menu in Page and the Post is the 'Page Attributes'. It allow us to select how overall Page or Post will look like. Di9erent themes of WordPress give di9er- ent options to us about the pages. Template option in it allow us to set page or post layout. Either we want to add left sidebar on a page, right sidebar on a page, etc. Let us see this menu's image:

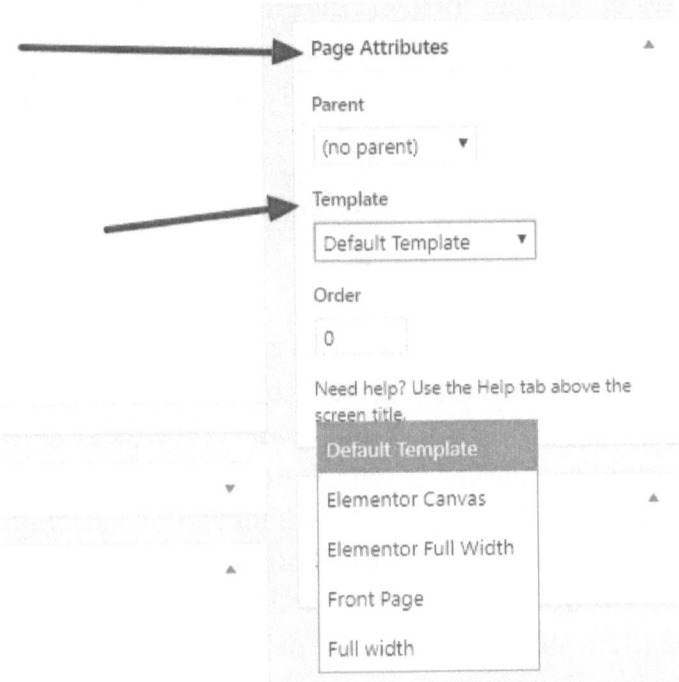

You can see here 'Page Attributes' menu. It allow you to set a Par- ent page name, Templates (this theme give option to set a default page template design, Elementor Canvas, Elementor Full Width, Front Page, Full Width. Di9erent themes allow di9erent Tem- plates, we can also make a custom template. We will study about WordPress Themes and Custom Templates (made by PHP and HTML code) later in the book.

5) Appearance: - Now let us study about Appearance menu.

Appearance menu has a lot of important sub-menus. Let us study them one by one.

a) Themes: - It allows us to select a theme for our website. When we completes the WordPress installation process, first thing we do after it, in WordPress is to install a Theme. There are a lot of free themes available in WordPress. There are also paid themes available. https://themeforest.net/category/wordpress?term=themes%20in%20wordpress#content is a famous site where you can search for paid themes related to particular topic. For example you want to make website linked to doctors, in search bar enter doctor theme wordpress and it will show you hundreds of relevant made themes with demos of each you can see. One of the demo is shown at this url: http://demo.ziscom.in here in menu you can select di9erent themes and pages. Most of these themes are also available to download free of cost on other websites such as https://themegrill.com/blog/free- wordpress-themes/ . You can search on https://google.com for free wordpress themes. Some of the most famous themes are Divi, BeTheme, etc. Theme is like a package of selected plugins and custom code done to make a website similar to the demo they show. You can simply change text and images in a theme and you get ready made website for yourself or to sell it. Each theme may include its own di9erent editor. All we need to do is understand the menus already made for everything.

It is always important to make a 'Child theme' after installation of theme. Many themes provide it or we can make a child theme through WordPress plugin or custom code. If our website get error, child theme saves it from going down by activating parent theme on it automatically. Menu shows various themes present in our list. And the active theme present in first number. When we click on 'Add New' button, as shown in above image, it opens page with a lot of themes:

Here 'Upload Theme' button allow us to manually upload a zipped WordPress theme which we downloaded from some other website. 'Search themes' text box allow us to search themes available from within the WordPress and install and Activate them through buttons.

Download themes are usually zipped inside the common folder which is also zipped. So we need to unzip it through Winrar software in our computer first. Check the readme.txt file etc. And theme present inside this folder which is also in zipped format, no need to unzip it. In WordPress we upload the zipped file dir- ectly.

Once the theme uploaded or installed successfully, it will show up in Appearance > Themes window. We can activate it by moving mouse on theme, and it shows the 'Activate' and 'Live Preview' button.

[i) Be careful when uploading nulled paid themes downloaded from other sites free of cost, they may contain viruses in them which may try to steal your data or show ads in your website.

ii) Many paid themes also need a key to enter which can be present in your readme.txt file or somewhere in the website where you bought it.

iii) We will study how to make custom theme, later in the book.]

b) Customize: - It is mainly a menu linked to theme. It opens in new window. It allow us to put logo of website, icon, tag line, footer, add custom css, etc. We can open it and go through all its menus to understand them. Di9erent themes show di9erent menus in 'Customize' page.

i) Additional css: - is a great feature present in it. It allows us to apply css (cascading style sheet) to change design of an element. Each page on website has a page or post id. We can see it by going to page and press Ctrl+Shift+I button or right click to select 'Inspect' element menu. First we give a page id, then the element id, class, name or path to apply css on a page element manually through custom code.

c) Widgets: - Widgets are also great features. Di9erent themes have di9erent widgets linked to them. On left half size of page, various widgets are shown and on the right half size of page various places are shown where we can drag those widgets to put them. For example a widget put in footer, will show those widget elements in footer of website. You can see in image below:

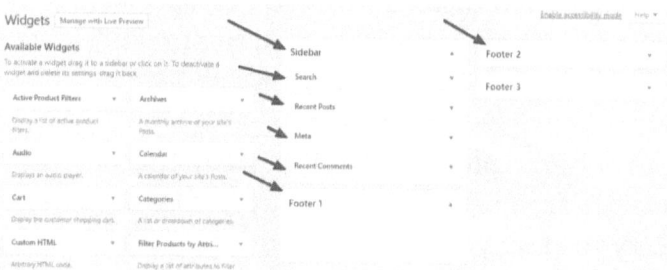

Left half size of page shows list of widgets. Right half size of page show areas like 'Sidebar', 'Footer1', 'Footer2', 'Footer3' where we can drag widgets and put in them one by one. 'Sidebar' shown above have four widgets inside it.

[We will study how to make custom widgets through code, later in the book.]

d) Menus: - We can create our website menus here. First of all we need to create a menu name. After that we put menu elements inside it from various pages, posts, categories, products, etc. we made or we can create a custom menu as well.

After that we create a menu structure as shown in image below. Main menu elements are placed on left, sub menus are placed below it and in the right. For example, Shop has two sub-menus, Cart and Checkout.

It could be possible that the Pages list above don't show some url which we want to add to our menu. So we can use 'Custom Links' for it. Let us study 'Custom Links' menu below:

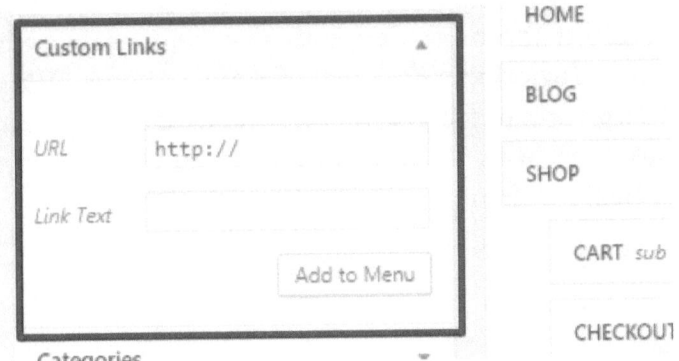

In 'URL' field, we can enter our URL and in 'Link Text' we can enter name of menu which will display. After that click on 'Add to Menu' button to add it to the right side in menu structure. By default, it get added to bottom of menu however we can drag it to anywhere inside our menu.

After menu is made we click on 'Primary Menu' option shown at bottom of page to make it primary menu for all website pages. And after that we click on 'Save' button to save this menu. We can click

17

on 'Delete Menu' link to delete the menu made, as shown in image below:

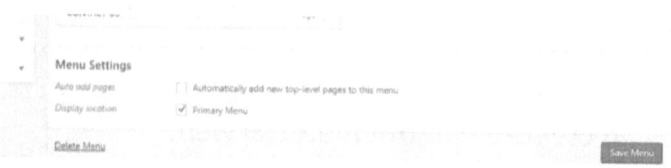

e) Header: - It opens the 'Customize' page. Here you can edit header menu of website.

[There are a lot of other menus shown here linked to the theme installed. Let us study the default and most important menu listed here - Theme Editor.]

f) Theme Editor: - It opens up a page which show list of themes and list of files linked to a theme, editable. One of the most important file to work in WordPress is func- tions.php file. If we have made a child theme for current theme, then we always do our code inside **functions.php** file of child- theme. We can not use normal php code in functions.php file as it is. There are some di9erences in code how we can apply PHP code in functions.php file however basic PHP methods remain same.

WORDPRESS HOOKS

WordPress coding mainly depends on hooks. Hooks refer to pre-defined working functions in WordPress. When those functions happen, we can add our code through hook to work with those functions. We can do database queries using $wpdb, make cron events and many other codes etc. Hooks are of two types:

i) Action hooks: - Action hooks are those which are used to add some action or function through our code when some function hits in WordPress. Let us see example to add 'Thank you for reading' in end of all our published Posts,

```
function my_text($content) {
  return $content . "Thank you for reading";
}

add_action('the_content','my_text');
```

In above example we have a 'hook' named 'the_content'. It is WordPress hook which is linked to WordPress Post content. We write the following code, to attach our function named my_text to this hook.

```
add_action('the_content','my_text');
```

Whatever output we want to run through my_text() function is displayed in function code as shown below,

```
function my_text($content) {
    return $content . "Thank you for reading";
}
```

In above function first we fetched all the content of the Post in

$content and returned $content with our own string after it i.e.

'Thank you for reading'. If you open any post, it will show 'Thank you for reading' written in end of all of them.

[Similarly WordPress has readymade hooks for many functions, we can search them in https://google.com for 'WordPress hook for doing this in functions.php'. We can attach our function with the hook.]

ii) Filter hooks: - It allows you to modify already made functions. Let us see an example in the Customizr theme. By default, when we click on logo of a Website, it leads to homepage. Let's change the url of the link in the logo:

```
add_filter( 'tc_logo_link_url',
    'change_logo_link' );

function change_logo_link()
    { return 'https://
    google.com';
}
```

Inside the Customizr core code, in the function that displays the logo (in class-header-header_main.php), Customizr has:

```
apply_filters(
    'tc_logo_link_url', esc_url( home_url( '/' ) ) )
```

This is where our add_filter() is hooking itself. The esc_url() func- tion eliminates invalid characters etc. in urls and the home_url() function retrieves the home url for the site. So without any filter- ing, the 'tc_logo_link_url' filter returns the home page's address.

[There are a lot of hooks in WordPress linked to plugins, themes, etc.. New themes and plugins are made daily so hooks are increasing. We need to search them on https://google.com, when we come accross similar tasks when we work on live projects. Noone can learn all of them, however it is important to know how to apply these hooks as shown in above examples.]

Other important file in theme editor is **footer.php** All the webpages has a common header and footer code. Footer.php contains the code which make footer. We need to edit it mainly because demo themes we download show footer with their text. We can edit footer from Appearance > customize menu, or through Appearance > Widgets. Sometimes it is not editable there and we can look in footer.php file. Footer.php file mainly contain hooks so it is not editable directly sometimes and can only be editted through Customize page. It depends on di9erent Themes.

It is mainly not recommended to edit files from theme editor or any editor inside WordPress directly because any error made here may cause the WordPress to stop working, which result in Theme Editor also don't show up, so we can not edit it to make correction. So it is recommended to edit WordPress files through FTP like 'Filezilla' software or through Cpanel > File Manager of website which can be seen after logging in to hosting server such as hostripples.com, bluehost, etc. whichever you are using.

g) Plugins: - A plugin provides a readymade functionality to WordPress. There are a lot of free and paid plugins available in WordPress. Plugins provide readymade functionality to us in the form of menus. We can select options in plugin to put a lot of new functionalities in our website. Image below shows the Plugins menu. It contains 'Installed Plugins', 'Add New' and 'Plugin Editor'. Similar to Themes, we can directly search, install and activate plugins available from within WordPress 'Add New' menu. Or the other way, we can search them on https://google.com and download from other websites, either paid or free plugins and then upload them using 'Add New' button. 'Plugin Editor' allow us to edit plugins similar to the 'Theme Editor' allow us to edit Themes.

Now let us study why we use plugins. Plugins can be used to do a lot of tasks depending on our need. Let us study some of the plug- ins to understand their need.

i) Duplicate WordPress Elements: - This plugin is used to add 'Duplicate' button in Pages and Posts so that we can duplicate them. It allows us to copy all design of a page and we can make new one similar to it by just one button click and then change text and add some other design in page to make a new Page or Post quickly. It can also be used to test our Page or Post code. If we find any error in our Page or Post, we can do testing on duplicate copy of it by adding, removing elements of page which can be possible reason of error and finding solution for them. It is mainly depending on menu options. Once the solution found we can remove duplicate page and put solution in our original Page and Post to solve the issue. This plugin can be used to duplicate a lot of other types of pages created in other plugins such as Woocommerce products, Popup maker, etc.

ii) Max Upload Size: - This plugin allow us to increase the maximum upload size of image or file we can upload in WordPress Media. We can lower the size through this plugin to restrict heavy files from uploading.

iii) Contact Form 7: - It is a very old and famous plugin. It allow us to make contact us form. You can see example of Contact Form

7 setup here: https://ziscom.in/contact_us/ . It allow anyone to enter their name, email, subject and message. And when a person enters 'Send' button, it automatically sends email to the Website owner with the message details.

When we Activate this plugin in WordPress, it automatically cre- ates a menu named 'Contact' in left side of WordPress menu. Contact Form 7 menu as 'Contact'. And we can make Form inside 'Form' menu shown inside it. We can set 'Mail' settings as shown in image. Once we save the form through 'Save' button we can see the code written in above picture in blue stripe.

[contact-form-7 id="29" title="Contact form 1"]

It is a shortcode. It is automatically generated code for this form. We can copy that code inside our WordPress Page or Post to dis- play our form there.

[If you do not understand how to make form in it through menu, its better to visit 'Contact Form 7' support links given in right side of page below 'Save' button (not shown in image above) or search https://google.com for it.]

iv) Woocommerce: - This is a very famous plugin to create E-commerce website or shop in the Website. It automatically creates Product menu in WordPress, where we can enter Product de- tails. It automatically creates 'Shop' page https://ziscom.in/shop/ which will contain Products made by us through 'Product' menu. It also sets up 'Cart' and 'Checkout' page. It also give us op- tion to set payment method, shipping method from within the Woocommerce menu. Any place order of product, can be seen through 'Order' menu.

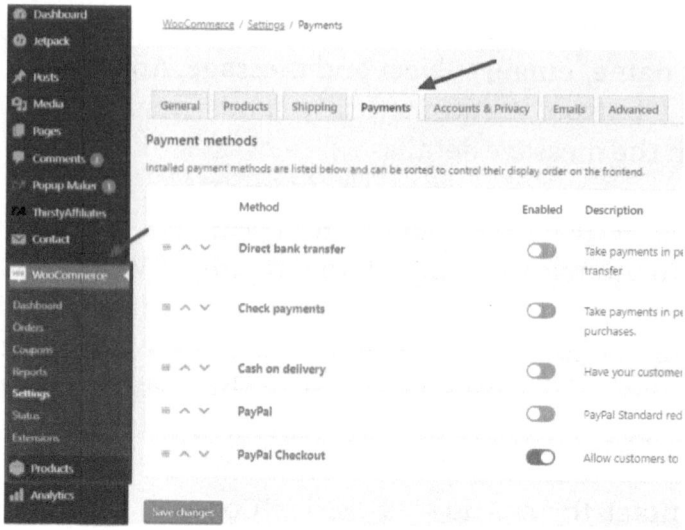

Image below shows 'Woocommerce Payment menu'. We can select payment options and can also add a lot of other payment options through other plugins.

We get a lot of options to set in these menus. In case of Woocom- merce > Settings > Shipping > Shipping zones. We can set shipping zones here for di9erent countries or famous cities and set flatrate, free shipping, local pickup options. 'Flat rate' refers to how much additional shipping fee will add to any order placed from this country. In case of local order, we can set it to 'free shipping' or 'local pickup' option when a customer place order through Shop page. There are a lot of other options we can set through these menus and they mostly cover everyone's needs. That is why this plugin is famous throughout World.

v) Buddypress: - It is a famous plugin which allow us to make modules for making a social networking site. We can create chat, blogs, etc. in our website through this website.

vi) Yoast SEO: - It is a famous SEO plugin. The main work of SEO plugin is to increase website traffic by optimizing our website. We can set options in its menus to make our site better. It also make sub-menus below each page and post to make them more easily detectable to google.com and easy to search by people, etc.

vii) Really Simple SSL: - It convert all website links from http to https however you need to set up SSL through host.

viii) WP Statistics: - This plugin allows you to check how many users visiting your website. From where traffic is coming, etc.

ix) Popup maker: - It is a good plugin to create popups on your website. There is need to understand the menu of plugin properly to use this plugin.

x) WP cache: - The plugin speeds up our website's load time.

There are a lot of other plugins within similar functionality and for many other functionalities. Some are not compatible with latest version of website. Some have very good feedback and some are highly used. We need to choose a good plugin for our website based on our requirement and plugin's feedback and number of active installs by users.

MAKE A WORDPRESS PLUGIN

We can also create our own plugin and get it published. Writing a plugin basically need two files. One is file with plugin code and second is readme.txt file.

i) Plugin main file: - On top of the plugin file we write this code in commented form, as shown below:

```
<?php
/*******************************
* Plugin Name: Name of plugin
* Plugin URI:   https://webpagelinkedtoplugin.com/
* Description: One line plugin description
* Version:     1.0
* Author:      Your name
* Author URI:  https://yourwebsitename.com
* License:     GPL2 or later
*******************************/
```

Below we write our plugin hooks and filter which do actual work.

ii) readme.txt: - Readme.txt file needs to be written in proper format. It also contains some important data on top of page, as shown below:

```
=== Plugin Name ===
```

> **Contributors:** (this should be a list of wordpress.org userid's) Donate link: http://example.com/
> **Tags:** comments, spam
> **Requires at least:** 5.1
> **Tested up to:** 5.2
> **Requires PHP:** 7.2
> **Stable tag:** 4.3
> **License:** GPLv2 or later

In above code === refers to <h1>, if we write == it refers to <h2> of html.

Below the above written code we write plugin description, Installation steps, frequenty asked questions about plugin, changelog, upgrade notice as shown in this page: https://wordpress.org/plugins/readme.txt

All the code written in readme.txt file will get fetched by the wordpress.org when we get our plugin published. This page shows how to edit images for our plugin, their names, their sizes, their format, etc.: https://developer.wordpress.org/plugins/wordpress-org/plugin-assets/

Once we are ready we can get our plugin published. For it first of all we need to create our wordpress.org account at https://login.wordpress.org/ after that upload your plugin to https://wordpress.org/plugins/developers/add/ They will email you if the plugin needs some correction or if it is good to go, etc.. Plugin with few files get approved quickly. Once the plugin get approved, we need to upload it on svn. SVN consist of four folders, assets, branches, tags and trunk. In trunk we put our main plugin. In tags, we make folders with name 1.00, 2.00. It is for di9erent versions of plugin. First version of plugin is placed in 1.0.0, later when we make changes in trunk folder for updates, it get placed in 2.0.0 and further changes in 3.0.0, etc. In assets folder we put images, videos linked to our plugin. Details about it are available in wordpress.org website at https://developer.wordpress.org/plugins/wordpress-org/how-to-use-subversion/#task-3 To upload our files to svn path received at our email address we need to use software. If you have Windows operating system in computer, you can use TortoiseSVN and if you have Ubuntu operating system in computer then you can use RapidSVN software to upload files to svn. Once plugin gets published, it is available to use by anyone in WordPress plugin directly. It may take few days to be searchable easily and all around the world web developers can use it free of cost. When you work on new plugins, it also get eas- ily accessible for you to use.

[Many developers put demo trial version of plugin in WordPress and paid full version in their website so that people from around the world can buy it. If you are good in coding, a one page plugin can be made in few hours and can get approved in a day. Complex and large plugins can take months or years to develop. Best way to edit a plugin is by downloading it in computer and opening it in editor software such as 'ATOM', etc. It allow us to search linked function names directly throughout the plugin to understand the functioning.]

h) Users: - Users menu in WordPress can be used to create di9erent kinds of users for our WordPress site. If you created WordPress, then you are set as 'Administrator' by default. Users menu has three sub menus,

i) All Users: - shows list of all the users.

ii) Add New: - Allows us to create a new user for website. One user can also register himself, if we have set it in our website.

iii) Your Profile: - This menu allow to set email, biography, password reset, first name, last name, address, company name, city, zip code, country, shipping address, etc.

We can edit a particular user to set it roles. Different roles have different powers. Different roles are, Shop Manager, Customer, Subscriber, Contributor, Author, Editor, Administrator. Different role set for a user give him different powers to work on website. Administrator has full access. Shop Manager can add, edit, delete products. Customer can buy products from website, Contributor, Author, Editor have different powers to work on Pages and Posts of website.

I) Settings: - This is the next important menu in WordPress. It is used to do a lot of settings in WordPress. It include many settings like setting homepage, blog page, It is shown below, media file sizes, permalink (or url structure), etc. Let us study its all sub-menus one by one.

i) General: - It includes some general settings of website such as website title, tagline, wordpress website url, email linked to website, new user default role, website language, timezone, date format to show in WordPress, time format etc.

ii) Writing: - It shows menu to set default post category, default post format when we create one, default editor (as we can install many types of editors like classic editor, gutenberg editor, divi editor, etc.), allow users to switch between editors or not, email settings, etc.

iii) Reading: - It alows to set which page will be website homepage (page which displays first), which page will be posts page (blog page) which shows all posts made, how many posts to show in a blog, show full text or summary of a post, is our website visible to search engines like google.com, etc.

iv) Discussion: - It shows various options and checkboxes we can select from for posts, comments settings, email, avatars for users made, etc.

v) Media: - It allow to set di9erent sizes of each image uploaded in Media i.e. thumbnail, medium or large.

vi) Permalinks: - It allows to set our url structure. For example, we want to show post id, or post name, or date of publishing, etc, in the url path for pages.

[As we add new plugins, they may hook in existing WordPress menu to add their menus for working purpose. We can use the menus to make our website. Website inlcudes, Page, Posts, media in our pages, themes, plug- ins, how to set homepage, how to set permalink, we have studied all important menus. We can make website based on this knowledge. Website mainly include menus, so working on WordPress require you to fix elements up or below logically to get the desired result rather than making logical structures in code.]

IMPORTANT FUNCTIONS

As we sometimes work on WordPress code, we come across some specialized code which is available to usein WordPress online. We can use these special functions for testing our WordPress code or making new functions. Let us study some of the important WordPress functions.

IMPORTANT FUNCTIONS

i) wp_mail(): - This function is used to send email through code. We can put it in our code within if condition. If the mail sent, it means function worked otherwise not. Let us see how to use it.

Simple mail function: -

wp_mail('myemail@mail.com', 'Subject', 'Message');

Above written is a one line email function, we can write email address to whom to send email, Subject of email and Message of email within 'inverted commans' as written in code above.

Complex mail function: - We can make a complex email with variables from our function, attachment, etc. Below is the example how to make complex mail function:

$mail = 'test49353@gmail.com';   /* write your email here, or

$admin_email = get_option('admin_email'); It is code to fetch WordPress admin email*/

$body = 'The email body content';

$headers = array('Content-Type: text/html; charset=UTF-8');

/* We can add header as UTF-8 if our message is in other language or below code (if required),

$headers = 'From: My Narme <myname@example.com>' . "\r \n";
*/

$attachments = array(WP_CONTENT_DIR . '/uploads/my-file.php'); /*my attachment file is in folder path public-html/wp-content/uploads/ which can be accessed through cpanel's file manager or FTP, etc. */

wp_mail($mail, 'Hi', $body, $headers, $attachments);

Above mail function is just using PHP variables to put in wp_mail() functions. We have defined these variables above.

[Despite from testing, we can also use it to send email to someone whenever a function is hit. We can send notification to admin or particular email if someone runs a particular function through frontend.]

ii) print_r(): - It is used to display data within an array. In WordPress data mostly come in arrays we can use print_r($arrayname) within our function, to print out our array in output page.

iii) exit, die():- It is mainly used for testing purpose. We can use it right after print_r() or echo to display contents and after that function will not run any more. We can use it as below,

```
echo 'abc';

print_r($myarray);

exit;
```

Above code displays text 'abc', array output and stops code because exit function written after it. We can also use die() function within our function. Benefit of die() function is we can also put our message in it as below,

```
print_r($myarray); die('It worked');
```

In case our array is empty, it will still show message 'It worked' in output and any code written after die() function will not work.

iv) $wpdb: - It is used to connect database in functions.php file of WordPress and extract data using MySqli query. Here is the example,

```
function myfunc($value)
  { global $wpdb;
  $wpdb->get_results(
  $wpdb->prepare(
  "SELECT * FROM {$wpdb->prefix}usermeta WHERE
  meta_value
  = '{$value}'"
  ));
  $wpdb->flush();
  }
```

Above we have a function named myfunc(), it is getting a variable $value. To connect to the database we used line:

global $wpdb;

After that we wrote code structure and put our MySqli query in it to fetch all data from table 'usermata' where column 'meta_value' has value '$value' which is dynamic data coming to our Word- Press function myfunc(), we can also pass a static value for $value within our function myfunc().

[To study in detail about MySqli and different queries, and database connectivity, you may buy our book 'Learn PHP' at https://www.amazon.com/dp/1693534835 It also contains a lot of other relevant knowledge required to learn PHP code methods which is basic of learning and understanding WordPress coding.]

v) add_option(), get_option(), delete_option(), update_option(): It many times happen that we need to add a value in our data- base table, later get it, update it or delete it. For it WordPress allow us to make changes to its 'wp_option' table directly using simple functions. Here is example how to use it:

add_option('variable', 'Done');

Above code saved data 'Done' in table column 'variable'. We can make new columns with different values in table 'wp_option' using above method.

Later we can get the value of column 'variable' using following code,

$x = get_option('variable'); echo $x;

Above code will display the value stored i.e. 'Done'. We can also change this value, update_option('variable', 'new');

Above code now saved data 'new' in table's column 'variable. We can delete this table's column and its value using following code:

delete_option('variable');

Above code will delete the column named 'variable', made in table 'wp_option' inside current website's database.

vi) How to make shortcode: - We can make a code and use it anywhere using a shortcode. Shortcodes are written in square brackets [ ]. Let us see how to make a shortcode in functions.php file,

function thanksShortcode() {

return '<p>Thank you for visiting us!</p>';

}

add_shortcode('thanksline', 'thanksShortcode');

In above code first we made a function 'thanksShortcode()' We have written text in it 'Thanks for visiting us!' inside HTML paragraph tags <p> and we have returned it using 'return' method. So whenever this function will hit this text will return or output. Below this line we have used WordPress function 'add_shortcode'. What this function does is it makes a shortcode named '[thanksline]' which shows output of function 'thanksShortcode' as written inside it. So if we put our shortcode [thanksline] anywhere in WordPress page or post, it will show the following output:

Thank you for visiting us!

Benefit of making shortcode is we can make readymade

structure of code for us, put it in the shortcode and use it at multiple places in our website with the help of one word shortcode rather than writing that code again and again. It saves time, space and also reduces complexity of code.

vii) How to make widget: - We can make a widget in WordPress and use it in Widget area in Widget menu. As studied before Widgets are present in Wordpress menu, **Appearance > Widgets**. When we install a theme it give us certain readymade widget areas, and widgets, however when we add new plugins, some of them may add new widgets for us which we may add in widget areas. Common widget areas are header, menu, footer, left sidebar of webpage, right sidebar, etc. Now let us consider we want to add something di9erent in the Widget area which is not provided to us in Widgets list. For it, we can make our own Widget in functions.php file. As we add the code, it will automatically get added in Widgets list and we can drag it in our Widget's area to add it in our website. Let us see how to make our own widget.

First we can create a simple widget using following code:

```
class my_text_Widget extends WP_Widget {
    public function __construct() {
        $widget_options = array( 'classname' => 'example_text_widget',
        'description' => 'This is an text widget', );
        parent::construct( 'example_text_widget', 'Example text Widget', $widget_options );
    }
}
```

In above code class name is my_text_Widget() and we write class- name and description in array $widget_options and in second half of code, we added array variable.

[It has many other variables we can put in it, we can study further about it at https://codex.wordpress.org/Widgets_API]

viii) cron: - Cron is used to set up timely events in our WordPress or to delay some function running. We can set cron to repeat an event hourly, daily, etc. Many times it happen that we receive data late in our function, so we can set cron to run a function when it get a particular value from database. Let us study simple example of cron first: -

```
function example_add_cron_interval( $schedules ) {
  $schedules['five_seconds'] =
    array( 'interval' => 5,
    'display' => esc_html_ ( 'Every Five Seconds' ),
  );
  return $schedules;
}
add_filter( 'cron_schedules', 'example_add_cron_interval' ); if ( ! wp_next_scheduled( 'my_cron_hook' ) ) {
  wp_schedule_event( time(), 'five_seconds', 'my_cron_hook' );
}
```

In above code we have made a cron which will hit after every five seconds automatically through 'bl_cron_hook'. We will show its implementation below however let us see how it is made above first.

1) First we created a function to make functionality of cron, named 'example_add_cron_interval()' which contains code for making cron for 5 seconds interval. This cron's name is 'five_seconds' and interval set is '5' which is five seconds.

2) Secondly, we added a filter hook, which adds our function 'example_add_cron_interval()' funtion's functionality to WordPress's default crons list which is 'cron_schedules'.

3) Thirdly, we added this cron's name 'five_seconds' to its actual name which we will use i.e. 'my_cron_hook' and added time() function to make it functional.

[It is a predefined method to create a cron hook. We can use our own time and variables in it to create hook for di9erent time however basic structure of code remains same.]

We have not added it to our function yet. We have not mentioned which function to hit after every five seconds, we can do so using add_action(), as shown below:

>   **add_action('my_cron_hook',
>   'sf_controller::sfp_myGenerator');**

Above code hits function sfp_myGenerator() function inside file sf_controller.php after every five seconds because 'my_cron_hook' function attached to it using 'add_action()'.

Now we can make it to run after five seconds, after a particular condition. Let us consider, we have added a variable, toggle_variable inside our function sfp_myGenerator(), whose value is set to 'start' on a particular if condition and once cron starts, we set it to 'stop' using our add_option and update_option function as studied in this chapter above.

We can use this code for it:

```
$cron_set = get_option('toggle_variable');
if($cron_set == 'start'){
    add_action( 'my_cron_hook', 'sf_controller::sfp_myGener- ator' );
}
else{
}
```

In above code we get value of toggle_variable in our variable $cron_set. Now if the value of $cron_set is 'start' then add_action will hit this function again using my_cron_hook otherwise not.

[We can search in https://google.com how to do something in functions.php in WordPress, how to connect database in functions.php file. It show us specific code which can be written in functions.php file in WordPress.]

IMPORTANT FILES

We can put our WordPress downloaded project directly inside public_html folder (in this case our website url directly opens website) or in another folder inside public_html folder (in this case our website opens inside our website url/folder name path). We will study important file and folders of WordPress here.

Important folders in public_html is wp-content. It also contains wp-config.php file, phpinfo.php, php_errorlog, .htdocs. php.ini file. Some of these files may be missing and can be generated through Cpanel menu as per requirement.

public_html > wp-admin
           > wp-content
           > wp-includes
           > php_errorlog
        > phpinfo.php
        > wp-config.php
        > .htdocs
        > php.ini

Inside wp-content folder multiple folders like themes, plugins, uploads, etc. themes folder contain themes present in website out of which we can use only one at a time. plugin folder contains data of all plugins installed in WordPress. upload folder contain all images, videos uploaded through WordPress menu.

wp-content > themes

> **plugins**
> **uploads**

Next important folder is themes, it contains list of our themes present in our website, by default there are three to four themes come free in WordPress installation:

themes > twentysixteen
> **twentyseventeen**
> **twentynineteen**

If we open any of this theme are important files:

twentynineteen > style.css
> **footer.php**

1) wp-config.php: - This file is present in our WordPress folder which is inside public_html folder. We can access folder through 'File manager' in cpanel or by connecting through FTP software (such as Filezilla). FTP can be created in Cpanel or in some hosts there is direct menu to make FTP login details which includes 'host name', 'normal ftp' or 'secure ftp sftp', 'username' and 'password', etc values which we can put in our downloaded FTP software such as Filezilla.

wp-config.php is a very important file. It has our database host, username and password details in it. We can also put our own code in it for increasing limits of website such as max_execution_time, we can set it to unlimited by adding following code in wp-config.php file.

@ini_set('max_execution_time', '-1');

It happens that sometimes, our some functions take longer time, however there is limit set by WordPress that if a function run longer than few seconds, then terminate it to avoid overload cre- ated by function, however if our function is important we can increate this limit of maximum execution time through wp-config.php file as explained above.

We can set it to display our Website's error messages by adding following code in wp-config.php file:

define('WP_DEBUG', true);

To hide errors, we can set it to false, as below:

define('WP_DEBUG', false);

or simply delete this code. We can create a file error log named php_errorlog in public_html folder which contains list of all errors using following code:

define('WP_DEBUG_LOG', true);

File created after this code added to is named error.log and is placed in our WordPress folder which is inside public_html folder or we can access it through cpanel menu directly to see errors of website.

There are many other Website options we can set in wp-config.php file which we can search on https://google.com online when required. Important ones has been listed above.

There are many other limits like post_max_size, upload_max_filesize, max_input_vars, etc, we can also set them in our other file php.ini present in our WordPress folder which is inside public_html folder or through Cpanel.

2) php.ini file: - This file is used to set limits. This file is present in our WordPress folder which is inside public_html folder if it is not present we can activate it through cpanel which will make php.ini file automatically.

3) phpinfo.php: - We can check already set limits on our website. We can create a new file in our WordPress folder which is inside public_html folder named something like phpinfo.php and put following code in it:

```
<?php
  echo phpinfo();
?>
```

When we open url ourwebsite.com/phpinfo.php then it display all the set limits and php version on our website, etc.

4) .htdocs: - It is a hidden file in our our WordPress folder which is inside public_html folder. All hidden files begin with dot '.'. We can also add a lot of important codes in it such as page redirects, page optimization code, etc. We have a lot of WordPress plugins available which can add code inside this file automatically for paritucular functionalities, or sometimes we open this file to delete some codes. This file is hidden and can be set to be seen by clicking Cpanel's settings and select option 'show hidden files'.

5) style.css: - This file contains the major CSS coding of website. We can edit it. We can right click on our website and click on 'Inspect' to see various elements and CSS applied on them. It can be edited in style.css file.

6) How to add text or shortcode output in middle of any page through footer.php file: - WordPress is a CMS and so is full of menus and if there is no option in menu to do something we can choose coding methods to get the work done. footer.php file is linked to all the pages in our website. We can use page id to point to particular page or post of website. We can add Jquery code in footer.php file and point to paricular class or div or id or section to point to it. When we add jQuery in footer.php file of our Word-

Press website we use 'jQuery' in place of '$' dollar sign. We can use this file to add custom text anywhere in our website through Jquery tricks, where sometimes we are not allowed to code directly in some precoded plugin codes or during some bug in Code or plugin. Here is the example of code how we can put Javascript code in footer.php file. We will see two example, first is adding dummy text in page, second is adding WordPress shortcode in a page.

a) Adding dummy text in middle of a page through javascript code in footer.php file: - First create a div in page where page id class is 'postid-1412'

```
<script>

var node2 = document.querySelector(".postid-1412 .single-product-content"), ele2 = document.createElement("div");

ele2.className = "my_gallery";

ele2.innerHTML = 'My text';

node2.parentNode.insertBefore(ele2, node2.nextSibling);

</script>
```

In above code, there is javascript code. First we selected an elem- ent whose class is 'single-product-content' this is in page whose page id is 'postid-1412'. We have created a new HTML <div> in it. We have set class name of <div> as 'my_gallery' and inside <div class ="my_gallery"> My text </div> we have put the text 'My text'. This above code have added a simple text 'My text' at per- fect location by making a HTML <div> element there.

b) Adding WordPress shortcode in middle of a page using PHP and Jquery code in footer.php file: - Javascript code do not directly fetch WordPress of PHP code inside its code, so we will do it indirectly in following two step way. It can be done in two steps,

a) Adding PHP code and then

b) Add Jquery, let us see below:

i) Adding PHP code: - In PHP we can select a page by its id in a different way

```
<?php
if (get_the_ID()==1412){

    echo '<div class = "mycodetrick">'.do_shortcode( '[myshortcode]').'</div>';

}
?>
```

In above code first we select page id '1412' using 'get_the_ID()' method. After that we made a HTML 'div' which have class name 'mycodetrick'. Inside this 'div' element we adding shortcode in WordPress way using 'do_shortcode()' and put shortcode '[myshortcode]' inside it. This code will add output of this shortcode in bottom of the page whose page id is '1412' in my website. Now we want to move this output to the exact location in the page. We will do it using Jquery code in footer.php file as shown below.

ii) Add Jquery code: -

```
<script>
jQuery(document).ready(function(){

    if(jQuery('.mycodetrick').length>0){
```

```
        var      gallery=jQuery('.mycodetrick').html();

      jQuery('.mycodetrick').remove();
    jQuery('.my_gallery').append("<div
    class='new'         style='text-
    align:center;'><strong>My    shortcode
    data </strong><br>"+gallery+"</div>");

  }

})
</script>
```

In this code first we checked that if there is any data in HTML element with class name 'mycodetrick' using method 'length>0'. If it has data then the data inside the element with class name 'mycodetrick' we put its HTML in our variable named 'gallery'.

After that we have removed (or hidden) the HTML element whose class name is 'mycodetrick' from footer of page.

After that we have selected class name 'my_gallery' of an HTML element in our page after which we want to move our shortcode data which is Jquery varaible 'gallery'. We made a div after HTML element with class name 'my_gallery', we gave this new div class name 'new' and using CSS style code we aligned it to center. Inside this div we entered our text 'My shortcode data' which is bold because of <strong> tags around it. After that we put break <br> tag to move next part of code in next line and using Jquery method of '+' we added variable 'gallery' to display all the output of shortcode here. After that we closed our div </div> as shown in above code.

[To learn Jquery in a better way how we can mix it up with WordPress you may read our book 'Learn HTML, CSS, Javascript and Jquery' at https://www.amazon.com/dp/B07Z68Z4RG . It contains a lot of linked topics which will help you a lot when working with WordPress as all these are also integral parts of WordPress code.]

[To understand chapter 4 and 5 study our books 1) 'Learn PHP' at https://www.amazon.com/dp/1693534835 and 2) 'Learn HTML, CSS, Javascript and Jquery' at https://www.amazon.com/dp/B07Z68Z4RG (you may also order PDF version of books if your budget is low.)]

CREATE CUSTOM TEMPLATE AND MENU

We can design our own webpage in WordPress through code. Benefit of coding in WordPress is we get readymade admin panel with a lot of inbuilt functionalities and for a single page we can code ourself because it is not always possible to create exact required functionality through WordPress editor. Custom code also help us create custom menus in WordPress to han- dle as per our requirement. To do custom code in WordPress it is important that you know PHP, HTML, CSS, Javascript, Jquery. To learn it from us, you may buy our other books i) 'Learn PHP' at https://www.amazon.com/dp/1693534835 and ii) 'Learn HTML, CSS, Javascript and Jquery' at https://www.amazon.com/dp/B07Z68Z4RG

Once you are ready let us study how to create a custom template first. First of all we need to design our page using HTML, PHP, CSS, javascript and Jquery codes as per requirement. After that we will put it in file structure of WordPress and mix it with WordPress menus using 'Custom Post Type' plugin.

MAKING PAGE TEMPLATE DYNAMIC

Now we will study how to convert page template dynamic. It take multiple steps:

a) Create Design of page through static code: - Here is a page's section code,

```
<section id="hero-section" class="hero-section"
    style="background:
url('FEATURED IMAGE')no-repeat center top /
cover">
  <div class="hero-overly"></div>
  <div class="biz-video-promo">
  <div class="container">
  <div class="row">
  <div class="col-md-7">
  <div class="biz-slider-text mt-60">
  <div id="typed-strings">
  <h1> TITLE <br>
  <span class="typed"></span></h1>
  <p> EDITOR </p>
  </div>
  <div class="hero-action-btn biz-video-overly">
  <a href="#service" class="page-scroll biz-btn-solid">Start Here</a>
  <a href="https://www.youtube.com/watch?v=LV3cjaA7NtE" class="video">
  <span class="ti-control-play"></span>
  </a>
  </div>
  </div>
  </div>
  </div>
  </div>
  </div>
</section>
```

Above code is a part of HTML body part. To make it work we also need to put links in head part of HTML as it includes bootstrap also. You can put TITLE as 'WE PROVIDE-', FEATURED IMAGE as any image path you have. EDITOR as 'Welcome to our website.' in above code. We will try to enter text dynamically for Title, Editor and Fea- tured image through WordPress menu.

b) Making a section of page dynamic: -

i) Selecting folder path: - First of all open your current WordPress's active theme folder in which we want to put customly coded template. Inside Cpanel or filezilla ftp software, you can find this folder in this path:

public_html/wp-content/themes/theme_name

Here 'public_html' is outer most folder and 'theme_name' is the name of the folder in which current theme's folders and files are. We will put file with above code and mix it with WordPress menus. You will find in this folder that header.php and footer.php files are already there because they come ready-made with the installed theme.

First of all let us create a file named template_home.php in our theme foder.

ii) Move <head> code to header.php and set current template: - In template_home.php file, on top of page we will write following code, to mix it with WordPress code,

```
<?php /* Template Name: Home */ get_header();
?>
```

and in bottom of template_home.php file we will put following code, to mix it with WordPress code,

```
<?php get_footer(); ?>
```

We did it, so that that HTML code's <HEAD></HEAD> section of this page gets code from header.php file and HTML code's bottom most code it fetch from footer.php file.

In between above code we put our designed page's code. However in our example we are only working on one section of web page. To make it dynamically editable from WordPress menu, we will install plugin 'Custom Post Type UI'.

iii) Setting links in header.php file: - Before installing plugin let us see how to put code in our header.php file, we need to edit all the links given in header.php file by adding following code after each href=" and src=":

```
<?php bloginfo( 'template_directory' ); ?>/
```

In case of meta charset code, make it as below:

```
<meta charset="<?php bloginfo( 'charset' ); ?>">
```

So our code links in header.php which are adding other css and script files will convert from:

```
<link rel="stylesheet" href="css/font-awesome.min.css" />

<script src="js/vendor/html5shim.js"></script>
```

to:

```
<link rel="stylesheet" href="<?php bloginfo( 'template_direc-tory' ); ?>/css/font-awesome.min.css" />

<script src="<?php bloginfo(
```

'template_directory'); ?>/js/ vendor/html5shim.js"></script>

So in our header.php file, below <head> tag our code will look like shown below:

```
<head>
<meta charset="<?php bloginfo( 'charset' ); ?>">
<meta name="viewport" content="width=device-width, initial- scale=1">
<link rel="profile" href="<?php bloginfo( 'template_directory' ); ? >/http://gmpg.org/xfn/11">
<!--favicon icon-->
<link rel="shortcut icon" href="<?php bloginfo( 'template_direc- tory' ); ?>/img/favicon.ico" sizes="16x16" />
<!-- font-awesome css -->
<link rel="stylesheet" href="<?php bloginfo( 'template_direc- tory' ); ?>/css/font-awesome.min.css" />
<?php wp_head(); ?>
</head>
```

Please remember to do above changes only in <head> </head> part of HTML code. header.php file may also contain some portion of <body> tag code which may include code for website menu, etc., so do not change the links mentioned anywhere in <body> </body> tags.

iv) Assign template to WordPress page: - Now let us see how to assign this template_home.php file to a WordPress page.

To do it first of all create a new page in WordPress. Now in 'Page attributes' menu select the template name. As discussed in point ii), we have set template's name as 'Home'. So select 'Home' and save the page. There is no need to write anything in this code. As we have set it to 'Template' as home, it will fetch page from our customly coded page.

v) Working on 'Custom Post Type UI' plugin: - Now let us see how to work on 'Custom Post Type UI' plugin. After installing and ac- tivating plugin, it will be available in left side of WordPress menu by name 'CPT UI'. Click on 'Add/Edit Post Types'. After clicking 'Add/Edit Post Types' it opens a new menu and form as shown:

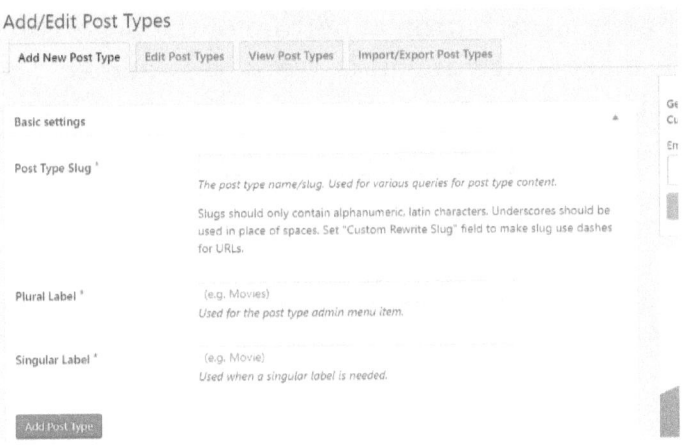

In 'Post Type Slug', enter the name of the url path which will be given to new WordPress menu. We can put in it relevant to our new menu we are making, eg. slider_home.

In 'Plural Label' enter name of menu. Let us name our new Word- Press menu as 'Home_main'.

In 'Singular Label' put the new WordPress menu name again which we are making 'Home_main'.

If we scroll down the page, it is actually a very big menu. As we scroll down the page, set 'Show in REST API' as 'False', as shown in image below:

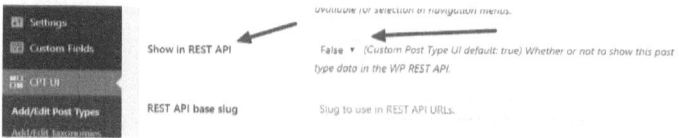

At bottom of same page, there is option to select which editables options we want to put in our new WordPress menu: We have selected 'Title', 'Editor', 'Featured Image', 'Excerpt' and 'Custom Fields' as shown below:

After selecting all these options, don't forget to save these settings by clicking the 'Save' button at bottom of the page. Once we made it, it will make a new menu is WordPress named 'Home_main' as shown in image below:

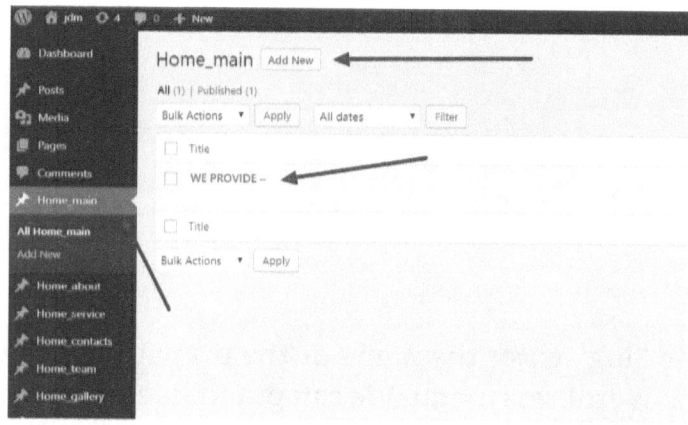

You can see in above image, it have made a new menu in WordPress named 'Home_main' and we can add new pages in it using 'Add New' and you can see we have created a page named 'WE PROVIDE -' using 'Add New' button. Now let us open this page and see what we can put there:

LEARN WORDPRESS

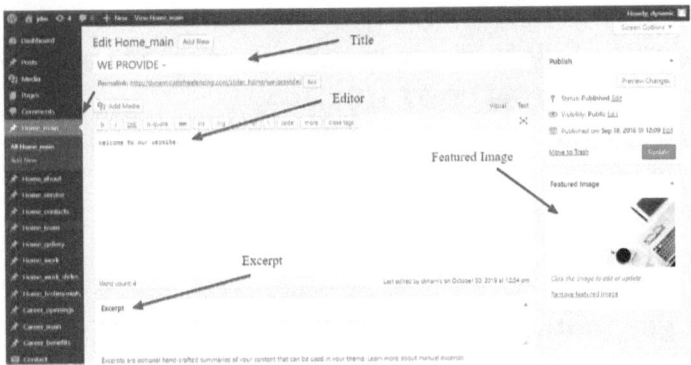

When creating a new menu, we have selected five options 'Title', 'Editor', 'Featured Image', 'Excerpt' which are present in this page. 'Custom Fields' option can be used with another WordPress plugin named 'Advanced Custom Fields' to add a lot of additional fields in our page. We will study about plugin 'Advanced Custom Fields' in next topic. Let us see how to use this made WordPress menu first.

'Custom Post Type UI' plugin gives us some code which we need to put around our designed code section's code as below:

```php
<?php /* Template Name: Home */
get_header();
?>

<?php
$args= array(
   'post_type' => 'slider_home'

);

$the_query = new WP_Query($args);
?>
<?php    if($the_query->have_posts()):    while ($the_query->have_    posts()):    $the_query->the_post(); ?>
```

55

```
<section id="hero-section" class="hero-section"
    <!-- SECTION CODE HERE -->
</section>
```

```
<?php endwhile; ?>
<?php endif; ?>
```

```
<?php get_footer(); ?>
```

In above code you can see, we have set 'post_type' => 'slider_home', where 'slider_home' is the name of our WordPress menu we have recently made using 'Custom Post Type UI' plugin.

You can see in above example, we have still kept header and footer code at top and bottom of our code. If we have more sections, we can make menus for them in using 'Custom Post Type UI' plugin and put same code as written above around our section and set 'post_type' as WordPress menu's name made using plugin. In this way, data entered in our menu will directly get fetched from our code. However what data will get fetched from 'Title', 'Editor', 'Featured Image', 'Excerpt' has not been explained yet.

In designed code of section, in place of **TITLE** put code:

```
<?php the_title(); ?>
```

So it will look like:

```
<h1> <?php the_title(); ?>
```

In designed code of section, in place of **EDITOR** put code:

```
<?php the_content(); ?>
```

So it will look like:

```
<p> <?php the_content(); ?> </p>
```

In designed code of section, in place of **FEATURED IMAGE** put code:

```
<?php echo get_the_post_thumbnail_url(); ?>
```

so it will look like

```
style="background: url('<?php echo get_the_post_thumb- nail_url(); ?>')no-repeat center top / cover">
```

By doing this our webpage will fetch code directly from Word- Press menu made by us through 'Custom Post Type UI' plugin.

vi) Working on Advanced Custom fields plugin: - To add additional custom Fields we need to add a new plugin named 'Advanced Custom Fields'. We can use it if we want to add more editable options in our designed web page through our menu. This plugin is used in combination with 'Advanced custom fields ui' plugin as explained through image in point v) above. To make it work we need to select 'Custom Fields' in 'Advanced custom fields ui' plugin. It allow us to make various other kinds of fields like dropdowns, date, image, check box, radio button, file upload, embed code, button, password, etc. After installing and activating 'Advanced Custom Fields' plugin, it adds in WordPress menu. When we click on 'Field Groups' sub menu of this plugin, it opens a page as shown in image below,

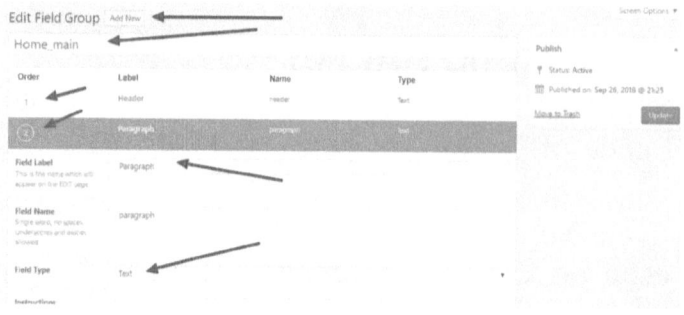

You can see on top of menu, there is option of 'Add New' to add a field. Below it there is field where we have written 'Home_main'. It is the name of the page section menu name which we have made in 'Advanced Custom Fields UI' plugin as explained in point v) above. Below it you can see we have made two fields' named 'Header' and 'Paragraph', where paragraph is shown in blue stripe and its sub menu is open. It give us a lot of options, to set 'Label', 'Field Name', 'Field Type' (where we can select to make it drop-down, checkbox, text, password, etc.), 'Instructions' (we can set some instruction about this menu), 'Required?' (we can set if this field is required or not), etc. there are a lot of other options in this menu (not all are shown in this image). When we save this, it will be available in our Home_main WordPress menu, as shown below:

You can see in image above two fields get added below 'Editor' section of 'Home_main' WordPress menu, which are named as 'Header' and 'Paragraph' as shown. We can put text in them and save the menu.

To link these fields to our code, we can add code in our file as follows,

Following code links to field named 'header':

<?php the_field('header'); ?>

Following code links to field named 'paragraph':

<?php the_field('paragraph'); ?>

As 'paragraph' is written above, it is the field's name. It is the field name we have set in 'Advanced Custom Fields' plugin. We can enter a field name within similar code and it will work out. What ever text we enter here, it will get fetched in our code and display in our output page.

It is a wonderful way in WordPress to add custom coded pages in WordPress CMS. Next time we want to work on our custom made page, we can just change text through made menu in WordPress, rather than going in coding part. And if we want to repeat simi- lar sections with di9erent text, we can just make multiples sub- menus in the menu similar to 'Home_main' and they will keep adding in serial in webpage.

MAKING CUSTOM CODED WEBSITE MENU DYNAMIC

Here we are discussing about a website's menu. We know thow that a website's menu is mainly at top of page and it is common in all pages of website. It contains link to different webpages of website. We can make this menu in WordPress through WordPress's menu 'Appearance > Menus'.

a) Menu through code: - Let us make a custom coded menu through bootstrap navbar code. We put this code below the </head> section in header.php file. It is because header.php file is shared with all other Website pages through simple code. We make menu in it once and it will be accessible in all our website pages. Here is the normal code first:

```
<!--start navbar-->
<div class="navbar navbar-default navbar-fixed-top">
  <div class="container">
    <div class="row">
      <div class="navbar-header page-scroll">
        <button type="button" class="navbar-toggle collapsed" data-toggle="collapse" data-target="#myNavbar">
          <span class="sr-only">Toggle navigation</span>
```

```html
      <span class="icon-bar"></span>
      <span class="icon-bar"></span>
      <span class="icon-bar"></span>
    </button>
    <a class="navbar-brand page-scroll" href="index.html">
      <img src="img/logo.png" alt="logo">
    </a>
  </div>

  <!-- Collect the nav links, forms, and other content for toggling -->
  <div class="navbar-collapse collapse" id="myNavbar">
    <ul class="nav navbar-nav navbar-right">
      <li class="active"><a class="page-scroll" href="#main">Home</a></li>
      <li><a class="page-scroll" href="#about">About</a></li>
      <li><a class="page-scroll" href="#service">Service</a></li>
      <li><a class="page-scroll" href="#work">Work</a></li>
      <li><a class="page-scroll" href="#pricing">Pricing</a></li>
      <li><a class="page-scroll" href="#gallery">Gallery</a></li>
      <li><a class="page-scroll" href="#team">Team</a></li>
```

```html
<li><a class="page-scroll" href="#contact">Contact</
a></li>
            </ul>
          </div>
      </div>
    </div>
  </div>
  <!--end navbar-->
```

In above code <div class="navbar-header page-scroll"> contains just login, link of logo, image of logo code and other code linked to website logo. Where path logo.png written, you can give path of your own image to put this logo in your menu. When this div closes, below the code of di9erent Navbar menus and their links to di9erent pages through href=" HTML method to add links.

b) Make above custom coded menu dynamic: - Now let us convert it to the code which will allow us to make a menu with similar design through WordPress menu 'Appearance > Menus'. We need to replace above static code in header.php file with following code:

```php
</head>

<?php $defaults =
  array( 'theme_location'
  => 'primary', 'menu'     =>
  'First_menu', 'container'
  => 'div',
  'container_class'     =>    'menu-{menu   slug}-
  container', 'container_id' => 'menu1',
  'menu_class'          =>
  'menu', 'menu_id'
  => 'nav', 'echo'        =>
  true,

    'fallback_cb'   => 'wp_page_menu',
```

```
    'items_wrap'        => '<ul class="nav
    navbar-nav navbar-right">
%3$s</ul>',
    'depth'             => 0
);
?>
<header class="header">
 <!--start navbar-->
 <div class="navbar navbar-default navbar-fixed-top">
   <div class="container">
    <div class="row">
     <div class="navbar-header page-scroll">
        <button type="button" class="navbar-toggle collapsed" data-toggle="collapse" data-target="#myNavbar">
         <span class="sr-only">Toggle navigation</span>
         <span class="icon-bar"></span>
         <span class="icon-bar"></span>
         <span class="icon-bar"></span>
        </button>
        <a class="navbar-brand page-scroll" href="index.html">
         <img src="<?php bloginfo( 'template_directory' ); ?>/img/ logo.png" alt="logo">
        </a>
     </div>

          <!-- Collect the nav links, forms, and other content for toggling -->
     <div class="navbar-collapse collapse" id="myNavbar">
```

```
            <?php wp_nav_menu( $defaults ); ?>
          </div>
         </div>
        </div>
       </div>
       <!--end navbar-->

      </header>
```

In above code, we put special php code, where name of menu is set to 'First_menu' using this code:

'menu'   => **'First_menu'**,

Rest of the code in variable $defaults written in PHP code is man- datory. We have also converted logo url with

`<?php bloginfo( 'template_directory' ); ?>/`

as shown in code above. Where our menu links were we have added following code there:

`<?php wp_nav_menu( $defaults ); ?>`

So it will fetch links through WordPress, while rest of the menu design gets made through our custom code. Once we make a menu in WordPress named 'First_menu' through 'Appearance > Menus' and add links in it. It will form the structure as made through our custom code.

API INTEGRATIONS

API integration allow us to join di9erent software application to our WordPress website. For example we created a contact form through 'contact form 7' plugin and we want that any person who fill this form, his data will automatically move to our con- vergehub.com website where we are handling all the clients. For it we need to do Convergehub API integration. Or we want that any person who fill the form, he automatically gets redirected to signrequrest.com website which allow to convert the form data in the form of a PDF file and on which a person can sign the PDF file through mouse cursor. For it either we use ready made plugins or we can get ready made custom code from the website. Many websites allow integration through a famous plugin like 'Zapier'. It can help us to write data in google sheets and data will be used to make new members in WordPress through 'Paid Membership Pro' plugin. Zapier allow a lot of different software application in- tegration to WordPress website.

In case you are more insterested in API integrations in PHP, I have published a separate book linked to Dropbox APIs integration in PHP, Javascript and HTML at: https://www.amazon.com/dp/B0DWT8BY2P with by line by line details, flowchart, alogrithms and examples of working project.

Following is the custom code to integrate convergehub API and signrequrest API in WordPress. Following codes are not explained in detail however working code for referencing working tested code.

CONVERGEHUB API INTEGRATION

Convergehub is used to get data filled in forms. To use Convergethub, we must have a paid account on convergehub.com and everything should be setup. Dummy Convergehub API integration code is also available here https://developer.convergehub.com/v2/update/#php however it is not functional. We will share a working code for Convergehub API integration to 'Update a lead'. You may also try Converge hub API integration 'add on' with 'contact form 7' plugin however it was a non-functional plugin as tested in August, 2019.

We can create a file in our public_html folder. We also need to add a script in footer.php file which redirect after 5 to 10 seconds to this page after clicking the final submit button of form. We can set form button's id through 'Contact Form 7' plugin form's code, which is accessible through WordPress menu. Add the following code in new file created in public_html to create convergehub API integration. Rememer to fill bolded important values in following fields, such database connectivity name, username, password and API integration keys. In this API we have di9erent fields however you may have di9erent fields in your website form. So please fetch the values accordingly from dadtabase to be integrated in convergehub API. This code is set to fetch latest database entry in form through 'Contact Form 7' plugin:

```
<html>
  <head>

    <script src="//ajax.googleapis.com/ajax/libs/jquery/1.11.0/jquery.min.js"></script>

   <script>window.onload = function() { if(!window.location.hash) {
   window.location = window.location + '#loaded';
```

```
      window.location.reload();
    }
}</script>

  </head>
<body>

<?php

    $servername = "localhost";
    $username = "ENTER DATABASE USERNAME";
    $password = "ENTER DATABASE PASSWORD";
    $database = "ENTER DATABASE NAME";

    $conn = new mysqli($servername, $username, $password, $database);

    $query0 = "SELECT max(entry_id) FROM `wp_rgpv_cf_form_entry_values`";
    $result0 = mysqli_query($conn, $query0);

    while ($row0=mysqli_fetch_row($result0))
    {
      $entryid = $row0[0];

    }

    $query1 = "SELECT * FROM `wp_rgpv_cf_form_entry_values` where entry_id = $entryid";

    $result = mysqli_query($conn, $query1);                        while
```

```php
   ($row=mysqli_fetch_row($result))
   {

     if($row[3] == "first_name"){
       $firstname = $row[4];
     }

     if($row[3] == "last_name"){
       $lastname = $row[4];
     }

     if($row[3] == "email_address"){
  $email_address = $row[4];
}

if($row[3] == "owner_phone_number"){
  $owner_phone_number = $row[4];
}

if($row[3] == "name_of_business"){
  $name_of_business = $row[4];
}

if($row[3] == "time_in_business"){
  $time_in_business = $row[4];
}

if($row[3] == "annual_revenue"){
  $annual_revenue = $row[4];
}

if($row[3] == "credit_quality"){
  $credit_quality = $row[4];
}
```

```php
if($row[3] == "what_industry_are_you_in"){
 $industry = $row[4];
}

if($row[3] == "street_address_of_business"){
 $street_address = $row[4];
}

if($row[3] == "aptsuite"){
 $aptsuite = $row[4];
}

    if($row[3] == "city"){
     $city = $row[4];
    }

    if($row[3] == "state"){
     $state = $row[4];
    }

    if($row[3] == "zip_code"){
     $zip_code = $row[4];
    }

    if($row[3] == "owner_date_of_birth"){
     $owner_date_of_birth = $row[4];
    }

    if($row[3] == "amount_requested"){
     $amount_requested = $row[4];
    }

    if($row[3] == "amount_deposited_last_month_"){
     $amount_deposited_last_month_ = $row[4];
    }
```

```php
    if($row[3] == "type_of_loan"){
     $type_of_loan = $row[4];
    }

    if($row[3] == "home_address"){
     $home_address = $row[4];
    }

    if($row[3] == "city2"){
     $city2 = $row[4];
    }
    if($row[3] == "state2"){

 $state2 = $row[4];
}

if($row[3] == "zip_code2"){
 $zip_code2 = $row[4];
}

if($row[3] == "annual_revenue"){
 $annual_revenue = $row[4];
}

if($row[3] == "credit_quality"){
 $credit_quality = $row[4];
}

if($row[3] == "management"){
 $management = $row[4];
}

if($row[3] == "social_security_number"){
 $social_security_number = $row[4];
}
```

```
if($row[3] == "approximate_ending_bank_balance_"){
 $approximate_ending_bank_balance = $row[4];
}

if($row[3] == "business_tax_id_number_"){
 $business_tax_id_number = $row[4];
}

if($row[3] == "social_security_number"){
 $social_security_number = $row[4];
}

  }
  /** Database integrity completed above **/

  /** Convergehub API integration below (Working) **/

  $base_url = "https://api.convergehub.com/v2/";
  $apiKey = "CONVERGEHUB API KEY";
  $apiSecret ="CONVERGEHUB API SECRET";
  /* It requires admin access to convergehub menu to get these values */

  function call_new($url, $type = 'GET', $postfields = array(),
  $headers=false)
  {
    $ch = curl_init();
    curl_setopt($ch, CURLOPT_URL, $url);
    $type = strtoupper($type); if
    ($type == 'POST')
    {
      curl_setopt($ch,        CURLOPT_POST,        1);
       curl_setopt($ch,CURLOPT_POSTFIELDS,json_enc
```

```
      ode($post-
   fields));
    }
    if ($headers)
    {
     curl_setopt($ch,         CURLOPT_HTTPHEADER,
      $headers);
    }
    curl_setopt($ch,
    CURLOPT_RETURNTRANSFER,                  1);
    curl_setopt($ch,  CURLOPT_SSL_VERIFYHOST,
    0);                           curl_setopt($ch,
    CURLOPT_SSL_VERIFYPEER, 0);
    $result = curl_exec($ch);
    curl_close($ch);
    return $result;
   }
   //create Method

$data     =     array(    'account_name'=>
 $name_of_business,        'first_name'=>
 $firstname, 'last_name'=>$lastname,
'email'=>
 array(
  array('address'=>
   $email_address,'primary'=>'1','opt_out'=>'0',
   'invalid'=>'0','verified'=>'1'),
 ),
'phone'=>
 array(
                              array('number'=>
$owner_phone_number,'type'=>'Other','extension'=
>'','pri- mary'=>'0'),
 ),
'Time       In       Business'=>
```

```
$time_in_business,
'annual_revenue'=>
$annual_revenue,           'Credit
Quality'=>$credit_quality,
'industry'=>$industry,
'primary_address_street'=>
$street_address,    'Apt   Suite'=>
$aptsuite, 'primary_address_city'=>
$city,     'primary_address_state'=>
$state,
'primary_address_postalcode'=>
$zip_code,
'Owner    Date   of    Birth'=>
$owner_date_of_birth,      'Amount
Requested'=>$amount_requested,
    'gross_monthly_volume_cstm'=>
$amount_deposited_last_ month_,
'type'=>$type_of_loan,
'alt_address_street'=>$home_address,
'primary_address_city'=>$city2,
'alt_address_state'=>$state2,
'alt_address_postalcode'=>$zip_code2,
'annual_revenue'=>$annual_revenue,
'estimated_credit_score_cstm'=>
$credit_quality,     'Management'=>
$management,

   'description'=>$social_security_number,
   );
   $relationship =
   array(
    'bean_id'=>'demo-e6bb-f534-9d14-593538822a4b',
    'bean_module'=>'contacts'
   );
   $postfields =
   array(
```

```php
'apiSecret' =>
$apiSecret, 'apiKey' =>
$apiKey, 'request' =>
$data,
'relationship' => $relationship,
);
$url = $base_url."leads";
$response = call_new($url, 'POST', $postfields);

?>

</body>
</html>
```

In above code, first of all we have fetched data from multiple fields present in our database, through PHP code. After that, we have put those fetched data in Convergehub API.

SIGNREQUEST API INTEGRATION

To make it work, first we should have paid account in signrequest.com website. Using below API code, we can transfer our form's output to create a PDF file which will have all form values already filled, in which a customer can sign. It is a complex procedure to create an actual PDF file first and do multiple settings on it so that it will work when we apply signreqest API to it.

Similar to Above API first you need to fetch data in variables through PHP code, which we can feed in Signrequest readymade API.

We can create a file in our public_html folder. We also need to add a script in footer.php file which redirect after 5 to 10 seconds to this page after clicking the final submit button of form. We can set form button's id through 'Contact Form 7' plugin form's code, which is accessible through WordPress menu. Add the following code in new file created in public_html to create signrequest API integration. Rememer to fill bolded important values in following fields, such as database connectivity name, username, password and API integration keys. In this API we have di9erent fields however you may have di9erent fields in your website form. So please fetch the values accordingly from database to be integrated in Signrequest template id. This code is set to fetch latest database entry in form through 'Contact Form 7' plugin:

```
<html>
 <head>

    <script        src="//ajax.googleapis.com/ajax/libs/jquery/1.11.0/ jquery.min.js"></script>

   <script>window.onload = function()
 { if(!window.location.hash) {
  window.location = window.location + '#loaded';
  window.location.reload();
 }
}</script>

  </head>
<body>

<?php

    $servername = "localhost";
    $username = "DATABASE USERNAME";
    $password = "DATABASE PASSWORD";
    $database = "DATABASE NAME";

    $conn = new mysqli($servername, $username, $password,
    $database);
```

```php
$query0          =   "SELECT max(entry_id) FROM `wp_rgpv_cf_form_entry_values`";
$result0 = mysqli_query($conn, $query0);

while ($row0=mysqli_fetch_row($result0))
{
  $entryid = $row0[0];

}

$query1     =     "SELECT   *   FROM `wp_rgpv_cf_form_entry_values` where entry_id = $entryid";

$result    =    mysqli_query($conn,

$query1);                while

($row=mysqli_fetch_row($result))
{

  if($row[3] == "first_name"){
    $firstname = $row[4];
  }

  if($row[3] == "last_name"){
    $lastname = $row[4];
  }

  if($row[3] == "email_address"){
 $email_address = $row[4];
}

 if($row[3] == "owner_phone_number"){
```

```php
    $owner_phone_number = $row[4];
}


if($row[3] == "name_of_business"){
 $name_of_business = $row[4];
}

if($row[3] == "time_in_business"){
 $time_in_business = $row[4];
}

if($row[3] == "annual_revenue"){
 $annual_revenue = $row[4];
}

if($row[3] == "credit_quality"){
 $credit_quality = $row[4];
}

if($row[3] == "what_industry_are_you_in"){
 $industry = $row[4];
}

if($row[3] == "street_address_of_business"){
 $street_address = $row[4];
}

if($row[3] == "aptsuite"){
 $aptsuite = $row[4];
}
    if($row[3] == "city"){
     $city = $row[4];
    }

    if($row[3] == "state"){
```

```php
    $state = $row[4];
   }

   if($row[3] == "zip_code"){
    $zip_code = $row[4];
   }

   if($row[3] == "owner_date_of_birth"){
    $owner_date_of_birth = $row[4];
   }

   if($row[3] == "amount_requested"){
    $amount_requested = $row[4];
   }

   if($row[3] == "amount_deposited_last_month_"){
    $amount_deposited_last_month_ = $row[4];
   }

   if($row[3] == "type_of_loan"){
    $type_of_loan = $row[4];
   }

   if($row[3] == "home_address"){
    $home_address = $row[4];
   }

   if($row[3] == "city2"){
    $city2 = $row[4];
   }
   if($row[3] == "state2"){
  $state2 = $row[4];
 }

   if($row[3] == "zip_code2"){
```

```
    $zip_code2 = $row[4];
}

if($row[3] == "annual_revenue"){
 $annual_revenue = $row[4];
}

if($row[3] == "credit_quality"){
 $credit_quality = $row[4];
}

if($row[3] == "management"){
 $management = $row[4];
}

if($row[3] == "social_security_number"){
 $social_security_number = $row[4];
}

if($row[3] == "approximate_ending_bank_balance_"){
 $approximate_ending_bank_balance = $row[4];
}

if($row[3] == "business_tax_id_number_"){
 $business_tax_id_number = $row[4];
}

if($row[3] == "social_security_number"){
 $social_security_number = $row[4];
}

    }
    /** Database integrity completed above **/
    ?>

    <!-- signrequest api below -->
```

```
<script>
   jQuery(document).ready(function($){
     $('#cover-spin').show(0);
     //setTimeout(function(){
       $('#cover-spin').hide(0);
       "use strict";
       !function(t,e,n,i){
            var s=function(e,n)
{t.SignRequest&&t.SignRequest.           loaded||
setTimeout(function(){t.SignRequest.init(e,n)},50)};
         t.SignRequest=t.SignRequest||{loaded:0,init:s};
                                                 var
o="https:"==e.location.protocol?"https://":"http://",u
=e.createEl ement("script");u.async=!0;
         var c=e.scripts[0];
         console.log(t.SignReques
         t);
            u.src=o+"cdn.signrequest.com/
signrequest-js/v1/sign-                      request-
js.min.js",c.parentNode.insertBefore(u,c),t.SignRe-
quest.init(n,i)}(window,document,{
          // this initial configuration is optional, may also
          be un-
defined
          subdomain: " // you could for example
initialize the li- brary to use a specific team
subdomain here
          }, function (SignRequest) {
            // this callback is optional, may also be
            undefined
              // SignRequest library is loaded and also
passed as first argument
            // execute your code...
```

```
//var template_form = document.getElementBy- Id('template_form');

//template_form.onsubmit = function (event) {
//event.preventDefault();
//var form_data = SignRequest.browser.serialize- FormAsObject(event.target);
// the template id can be found in the link visible when editing a template and clicking the
// 'Show public signing link' button.
// this example template has a template tag with the external_id: 'city'.
var prefill_tags = [
    {external_id: 'merchant_legal_ name', text: '<?php echo $firstname." ".$lastname; ?>'},
    //{external_id: 'type_of_entity_ corporation', checkbox_value: true},
    //{external_id: 'type_of_entity_ general_p', checkbox_value: true},
    //{external_id: 'funding_id', text: '989696'},
    {external_id: 'sq_entity_type', text: '<?php echo $type_of_loan; ?>'},
    //{external_id: 'dba', text: 'administrator'},
    {external_id: 'business_phone', text: '<?php echo $owner_phone_number; ?>'},
    {external_id: 'physical_address', text: '<?php echo $street_address; ?>'},
```

{external_id: 'city_state_zip1', text: '<?php echo $aptsuite." ".$city." ".$state." ".$zip_code; ?>'},
//{external_id: 'business_fax', text: '785425'},
{external_id: 'mailing_billing_ad-dress', text: '<?php echo $home_address; ?>'},
{external_id: 'city_state_zip2', text: '<?php echo $city2." ".$state2." ".$zip_code2; ?>'},
//{external_id: 'bt_product', text: 'test product'},
// {external_id: 'bt_product_org', text: 'test org'},
//{external_id: 'bt_product_date', text: '12/1999'},
// {external_id: 'bt_product_length_of_ownship', text: '200'},
//{external_id: 'use_of_processed', text: 'ok'},
//{external_id: 'b_contact_name', text: 'abc'},
//{external_id: 'b_possition', text: 'owner'},
{external_id: 'b_email', text: '<?php echo $email_address; ?>'},
// {external_id:

'b_web_address', text: 'xyz.com'},
//
{external_id: 'b_funding_amount', text: '78500'},
{external_id: 'owner_name', text: '<?php echo $firstname." ". $lastname; ?>'},
{external_id: 'title', text: '78500'},
{external_id: 'social_security_name', text: '78500'},
{external_id: 'dob', date_value: '<? php echo $owner_date_of_birth; ?>'},
/*{external_id: 'owner_ship', text: '33%'},
{external_id: 'driving_license', text: '789532HH'},
{external_id: 'home_phome', text: '7896541236'},
{external_id: 'cell_phone_number', text: '7896541236'},
{external_id: 'marcent_email', text: '7896541236'},
{external_id:

'parmat_address', text: 'Fill the address'},

{external_id: 'city_state_zip3', text: 'new york,AK,10001'},

{external_id: 'owner_name2', text: 'new york,AK,10001'},

{external_id: 'title2', text: '78500'},

{external_id: 'social_security_name2', text: '78500'},

{external_id: 'dob2', date_value: '12/12/1993'},

{external_id: 'owner_ship2', text: '33%'},

{external_id: 'driving_license2', text: '789532HH'},

{external_id: 'home_phome2', text: '7896541236'},

{external_id: 'cell_phone_number2', text: '7896541236'},

{external_id: 'marcent_email2', text: '7896541236'},

{external_id:

'parmat_address2', text: 'Testing mailing address'},
{external_id:

'city_state_zip4',
text: 'new york,AK,10001'},
{external_id:

'card_Swipe', text:
'10'},
{external_id: 'manual_key', text:
'10'},
{external_id:

'mail_order', text:
'10'},
{external_id: 'internet', text: '10'},
{external_id: 'gross_monthly_sale',
text: '78888'},
{external_id: 'seasonal_yes', check-
box_value: true},

{external_id: 'seasonal_no', check-
box_value: false},
{external_id: 'jan_month', check-
box_value: true},
{external_id: 'feb_month', check-
box_value: true},
{external_id:

'march_month',
checkbox_value: true},
{external_id: 'apr_month', check-
box_value: true},
{external_id: 'may_month', check-

box_value: true},

{external_id: 'jun_month', checkbox_value: true},

{external_id: 'july_month', checkbox_value: true},

{external_id: 'aug_month', checkbox_value: true},

{external_id: 'sep_month', checkbox_value: true},

{external_id: 'oct_month', checkbox_value: true},

{external_id: 'nov_month', checkbox_value: true},

{external_id: 'dec_month', checkbox_value: true},

{external_id: 'terminal', text: '78888'},

{external_id: 'soft_ware', text: 'dos'},

{external_id: 'soft_ware_contact', text: '78888'},

{external_id: 'bi_funding', checkbox_value: true},

{external_id: 'bi_funding_company', text: 'dos'},

{external_id:

'bi_funding_taken_out', text: 'dos'},*/

{external_id: 'bi_funding_balance', text: '<?php echo $approximate_ending_bank_balance; ?>'},

/*{external_id: 'bi_behind', checkbox_value: true},

{external_id: 'utility', text: '14522'},*/

{external_id: 'bi_tax', text: '<?php echo $business_tax_id_number; ?>'},

{external_id: 'bi_liquor', text: '<? php echo $social_security_number; ?>'},

{external_id: 'rent', text: '78555'},

{external_id: 'bank_loan', text: '<? php echo $annual_revenue; ?>'},

/*{external_id: 'federal', checkbox_value: true},

{external_id: 'federal_detail', text: '78555'},

{external_id: 'bank_ruptacy', checkbox_value: true},

{external_id: 'bank_ruptacy_detail', text: '78555'},

{external_id: 'law_suit', checkbox_value: true},
{external_id: 'law_suit_detail', text: 'test law_suit_detail'},
{external_id: 'trade_ref1', text: 'test law_suit_detail'},
{external_id: 'trade_ref1_account', text: '784525852'},
{external_id: 'trade_ref1_phone', text: '784525852'},
{external_id: 'trade_ref2', text: 'test law_suit_detail'},
{external_id: 'trade_ref2_account', text: '784525852'},
{external_id: 'trade_ref2_phone', text: '784525852'},*/
{external_id: 'business_property_type', text: '<?php echo $name_of_business; ?>'},
/
*{external_id:

```
                    'business_proper-
ty_lease_team', text: '1'},
                    {external_id:

                    'business_proper-
ty_rent', text: '20000'},
                    {external_id: 'business_property_
building', text: '200sqt.'},*/
                    {external_id:

                    'current_date',
date_value: new Date() },

            ];
        //console.log('Using    prefill_tags:    ',
        prefill_tags);              vartab    =
        SignRequest.browser.signTem-
plate('ENTER TEMPLATE ID', {
            email:        '<?php      echo
            $email_address; ?>', next: '/en/
            example-signed/',   prefill_tags:
            prefill_tags
            });
            tab.onAny(function

            (event_type,   payload,
event) {
            console.log(event_type, payload, event);
            //console.log('o'+"hi "+'s');
            });
        return false;
    //};
    });

    //}, 12000);
```

```
        });

    </script>
<!-- signrequest api end -->
</body>
</html>
```

THANK YOU

www.ingramcontent.com/pod-product-compliance
Lightning Source LLC
Chambersburg PA
CBHW020559220526
45463CB00006B/2376